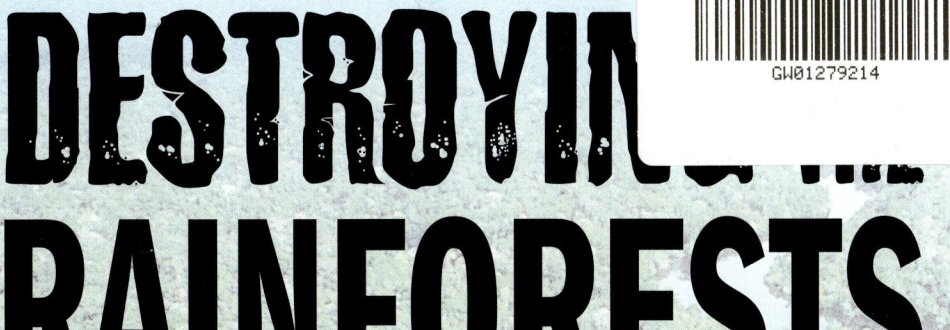

DESTROYING THE RAINFORESTS

James Driver

OXFORD UNIVERSITY PRESS

Contents

The rainforests 4
Trees and plants 6
Animals, birds and insects 12
Rainforest people 16
Loggers and farmers.................... 18
Why are rainforests important?....... 20
What do you think? 22
Index 24

The rainforests

Rainforests are hot, wet places, full of big trees, flowers, birds, insects and animals. They are found near the Equator, which stretches round the middle of the Earth.

World map showing rainforests

Rainforests used to cover whole countries, but they are being destroyed. Their trees are being cut down for timber or to make room for farms.

If we carry on cutting down the rainforests, they will disappear in less than 100 years.

This book will tell you more about the rainforests and why they are being cut down. Different people have different views on the rainforests. Think about them and then make up your own mind.

▲ This rainforest in Sumatra, Indonesia, is being cut down to make room for farms.

FACT BOX

Every second, an area of rainforest the size of a football pitch is cut down.

Trees and plants

Rainforests are the sunniest and wettest places on Earth. This means they are like giant greenhouses – perfect for growing trees and plants.

The rainforest has many layers. The tallest trees can grow to 60 metres. The canopy is like a leafy roof and many birds and animals live there. Young trees sprout up inside the forest. On the ground, ferns, fungus and some flowers grow.

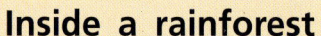
Inside a rainforest

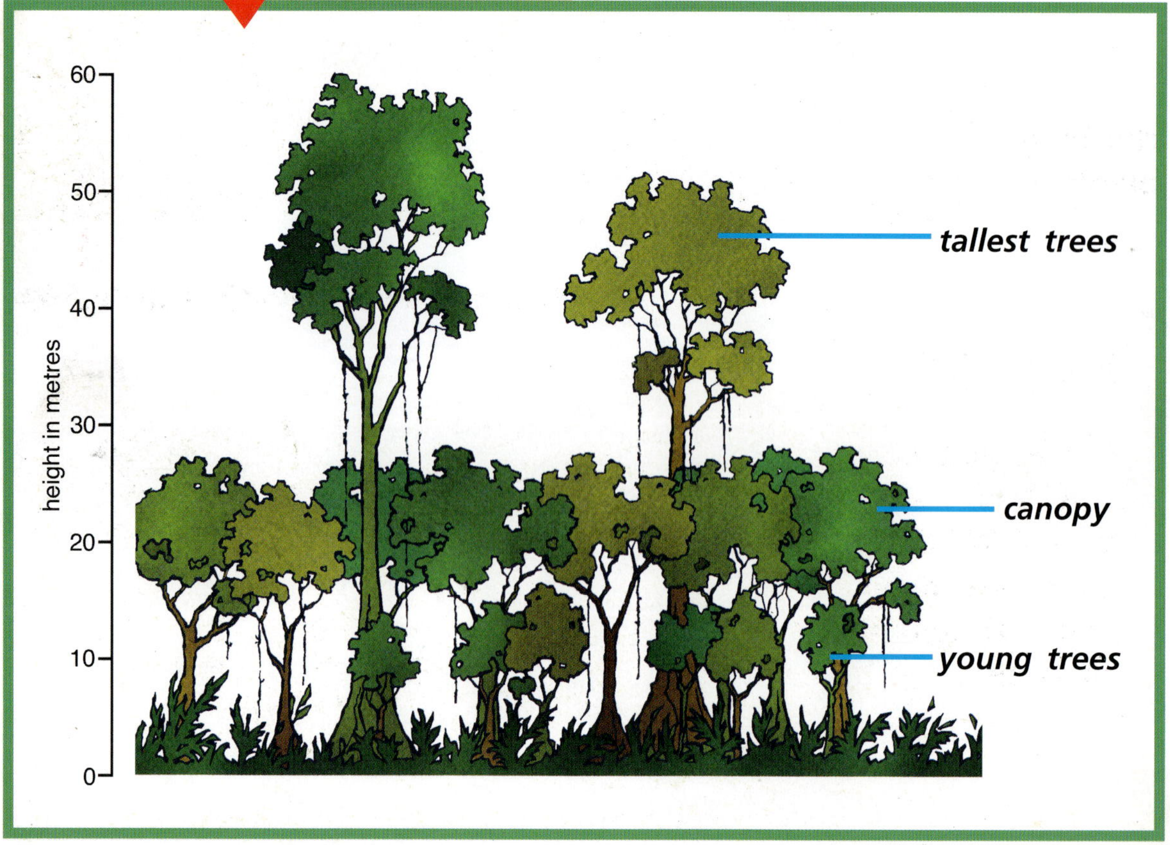

Trees grow to a huge size in the rainforests. Their roots spread wide to support the thick trunks. Some of their roots are above the ground because they get water from the damp air rather than from the ground.

climbing plants

"buttress" roots support the trunk

FACT BOX

In an area of rainforest the size of a football pitch, there are over 100 different kinds of trees.

The big trees support many other plants. Plants such as ferns and orchids root into the dirt that collects on the trees.

Strangler plants wrap their roots around trees, then grow down into the ground. They eventually kill the old tree.

old tree

strangler plant

This strangler fig tree almost covers the old tree.

Inside the rainforests it can be quite dark. The leaves block out the sunlight. Lianas trail down from tree branches. Their roots are in the ground.

lianas

Dead leaves and old wood rot on the ground. Fungus grows on them.

Fungus helps to rot old wood quickly and it is food for small animals.

Flowers in the forest are brightly coloured. They need to attract birds and insects to carry their pollen, as there is no wind.

This flower is called the "Flame of the Forest".

Some plants grow on tree trunks. They use their roots to hold on to the tree.

The Rafflesia is the largest flower on Earth. It can grow over one metre across. When it starts to decay, it smells of rotten fish!

◄ A Rafflesia flower

Pitcher plants eat insects and small animals. When the animals go to feed on the plant, they slip down the steep sides inside the plant. They cannot get out again so they are trapped.

A pitcher plant ►

Animals, birds and insects

A rainforest is packed full of millions of animals, birds and insects.

The leafy canopy is like a small city full of creatures.

Hummingbirds use their long beaks to drink nectar from rainforest flowers.

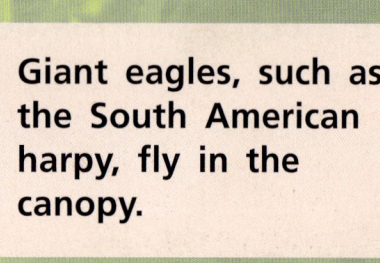

Giant eagles, such as the South American harpy, fly in the canopy.

Giant bees build nests high up in the trees. Only the bravest animals reach the sweet honeycomb.

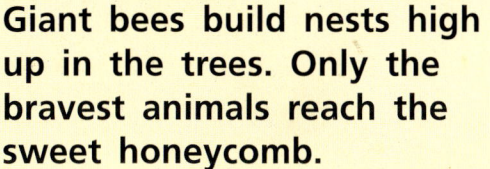

Animals like this giant flying squirrel have small wings to help them glide from tree to tree.

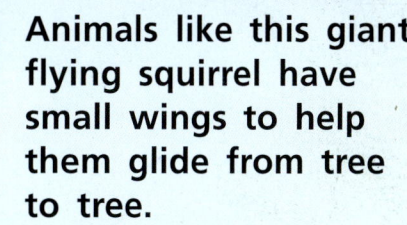

This orang-utan is a great ape. Almost all the great apes left on Earth live in rainforests.

Deep inside the forest are insects and reptiles.

Some frogs have skins that ooze deadly poison. Their bright colours warn off other animals.

Many animals camouflage themselves so they are tricky to spot.

This grasshopper blends into the colours of the branch.

Tiny insects, like these termites, feed off rotting wood on the forest floor.

Giant snails eat fungus on tree trunks, or dead wood.

Rainforest people

People have lived in the rainforests for thousands of years. They eat the fruits and the nuts that grow there. They hunt the animals. They make homes among the trees and grow vegetables. These people live in the rainforests without damaging it.

Some rainforest people hunt animals with blow pipes.

Many rainforest tribes still enjoy old ceremonies.

Rainforest people know how to make medicines from plants, how to get water from lianas, and how to use fibres from plants for making things.

Making baskets from plant fibres.

Children help to collect food.

Loggers and farmers

Many rainforests are in poor countries. These countries can make money by cutting down trees and selling their timber. The money can be used to build schools and hospitals.

Loggers are paid by big companies to cut down the trees.

Roads are built so the logs can be taken out of the rainforest.

Farmers cut down trees to clear land for their farms. They need land to graze cattle and grow crops.

First they cut down the biggest trees. Then they light fires to clear the land.

FACT BOX

On 9th September 1987, there were 7,603 fires burning in the South American rainforest.

Why are rainforests important?

Some people think the world is in danger of getting too hot. This is because gas from car engines, factories and houses goes up into the air and makes a layer that stops the heat of the sun escaping. This is called the Greenhouse Effect.

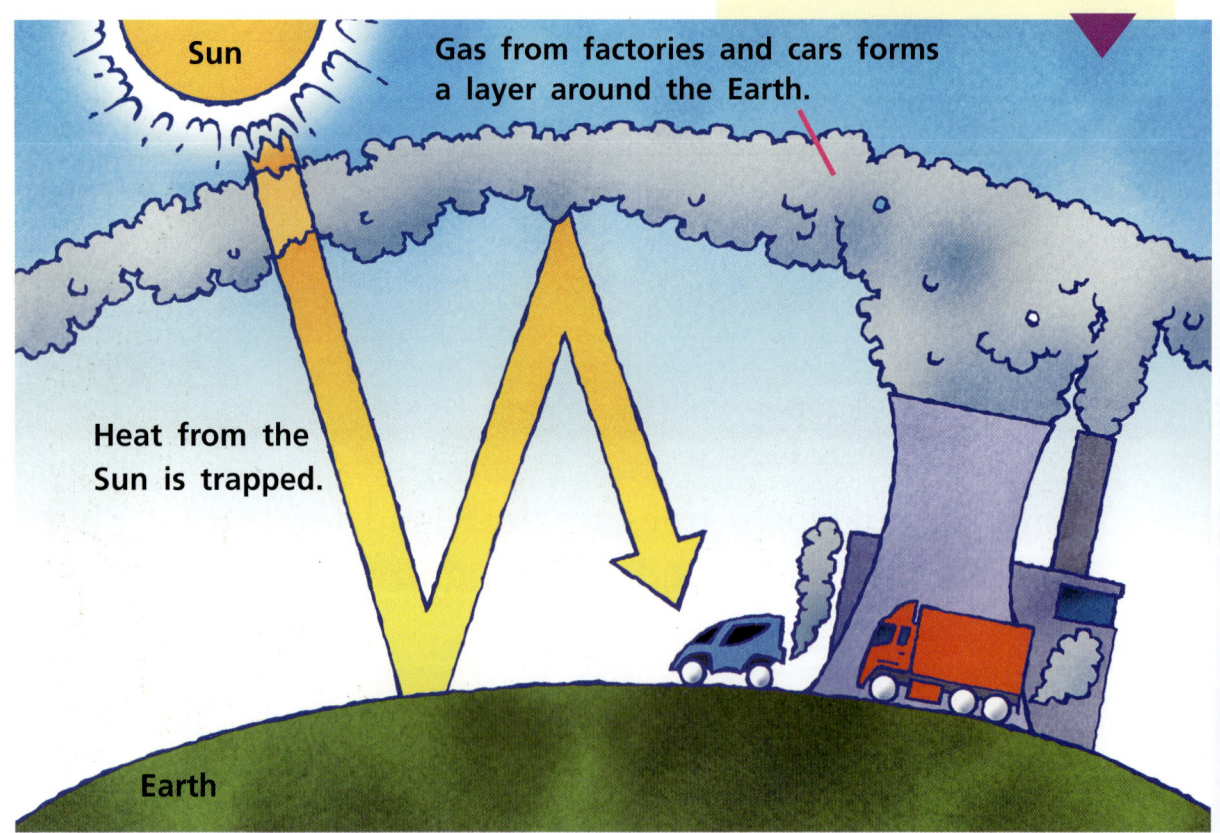

The Greenhouse Effect

Sun

Gas from factories and cars forms a layer around the Earth.

Heat from the Sun is trapped.

Earth

The rainforest trees take in some of the gas and change it to oxygen. If the trees are cut down there will be less oxygen. The world will be hotter and less healthy.

Many medicines come from rainforest plants.

The bark of the cinchona tree can be used to make quinine to treat malaria.

Rainforest people use curare, from lianas, to poison the tips of their weapons. Doctors use it too, to relax patients' muscles.

FACT BOX

So far, more than 2,000 rainforest plants have been found that can help people who have cancer.

What do you think?

The destruction of the rainforests affects many people. They all have different views.

Rainforest people
If the rainforests are destroyed we will lose our whole way of life. We have lived in the rainforests for thousands of years without damaging them.

Loggers
Big companies pay us good money for timber. They bring roads and new technology to the rainforests. More money helps pay for schools and hospitals.

Scientists
If we lose the rainforests and all their plants, we will lose the chance to find cures for many more diseases. So we think the rainforests should be saved.

Farmers

We need land to grow crops and graze cattle, so we need to clear the land. We have a right to earn our living as farmers.

Environmentalists

We need the rainforests to keep the world healthy. If they go, the climate may change and many parts of the world may flood.

Governments of poor countries

We have a right to develop our countries and get more money to spend on our people. The richer countries should pay us if they want us to keep the rainforests.

Index

bees   13
canopy   6, 12
cattle   19, 23
crops   19, 23
eagles   12
farms   4, 19
fires   19
flowers   4, 6, 10, 11, 12
frogs   14
fungus   6, 9, 15
Greenhouse Effect   20
hummingbirds   12
insects   4, 10, 11, 12–15
lianas   9, 17
loggers   18, 22
medicines   17, 21
orang-utan   13
rainforest people   16–17, 21, 22
roads   18, 22
roots   7, 8, 9, 10
snails   15
squirrel   13
strangler plants   8
termites   15
timber   4, 18, 22
water   7, 17